MW01618006
Riddell
4
NFL
Wilson
NFL

Riddell
NFL
NFL

BRETT FAVRE

RICHARD J. BRENNER

AN EAST END PUBLISHING BOOK
SYOSSET, NY

Brett Lorenzo Favre, who was born in 1969, grew up as part of a tightly knit family in the tiny town of Kiln, Mississippi. Brett and his two brothers, Scott and Jeff, loved playing in the family's backyard.

But they always had to be careful about getting too close to Rotten Bayou, a stretch of water that is home to *lots* of alligators.

When Brett played his games of backyard football, he'd sometimes pretend that he was Roger Staubach, who quarterbacked the Dallas Cowboys to a pair of Super Bowl victories in the 1970s.

Wilson

At other times he'd pretend to be Archie Manning, who was the quarterback of the New Orleans Saints. Brett loved scrambling around the backyard while pretending that he was scampering around the Louisiana Superdome.

"I always loved the magic of being a kid, the feeling that anything is possible," says Brett, who began dreaming of becoming a National Football League quarterback when he was in the sixth grade.

Brett had started playing organized football the year before, as a wide receiver. But after he fell on the ball and had the wind knocked out of him, he asked to be switched to quarterback.

"Suddenly, it was like a jamboree," recalls Brett. "I threw like three touchdown passes, and ran for maybe three more. Right then, I said to myself, 'This is for me.' "

PACKERS
NFL
4

Brett went on to become the quarterback for his high school team, where his father, Irvin, was the coach. Unfortunately for Brett, his dad favored the running game over the passing game.

Because he threw so few passes, Brett didn't have much of a chance to impress college coaches. "I was never recruited by a college," says Brett. "No one really wanted me."

Wilson
NFL

Luckily, Brett finally did receive a scholarship from the University of Southern Mississippi, but only after another player decided to go to a different college.

Although Brett was only a seventh stringer when he arrived at USM, he surprised everybody by becoming a record-breaking, four-year starter for the Golden Eagles.

Riddell
Wilson

"I wasn't the most gifted athlete," says Brett. "Both my brothers were better high school players than I was. So I always knew that I had to work harder."

4

Brett began his NFL career in 1991 with the Atlanta Falcons, but was traded to Green Bay before the start of the 1992 season. "I just really liked him," said Packers' general manager Ron Wolf. "I thought he would be special."

Brett has gone on to prove that Wolf knew *exactly* what he was talking about by becoming the only player in league history to win three MVP awards. And he's also led the Packers to an awesome win in Super Bowl XXXI.

"Even though I've finally realized my dream," says Brett, "sometimes I have to pinch myself when I think there's a little kid somewhere who's running around saying, 'I'm Brett Favre.' "

ISBN 0-943403-56-1 • Printed in the United States of America. • This book is not authorized by Brett Favre.

Book Design and Layout: Eric Macaluso

Photo Credits: **SPORTSCHROME** supplied the following photos: Large cover, as well as pages 3, 24, and 32 were taken by **Vincent Manniello**; page 12 by **Michael Zito;** page 21 by **John Williamson**; the small photo in the center of the cover was taken by **Rob Tringali, Jr.** Page 31 was supplied by **ALLSPORT USA,** and taken by **Scott Halleran.** All of the other cover and interior photos were taken and supplied by **Tony Inzerillo.**

Thanks to Judy Newman and Liz Loftus.

Riddell
NFL
4